JAPAN
The Ancient
Rice Fields

JAPAN
The Ancient Rice Fields

Photographs and Text by
Johnny Hymas

SHUFUNOTOMO CO., LTD.
Tokyo, Japan

To Shun Kamiya

Art Direction by Toshiaki Suzuki

Johnny Hymas Photo Office
4274 Minami Yamada-cho
Tsuzuki-ku, Yokohama City
Kanagawa Prefecture
224-0026 Japan
Tel & Fax 81-45-593-0059
http://www.johnny-hymas.net/
e-mail: photo-office@johnny-hymas.net

First printing, 2001

Published by Shufunotomo Co., Ltd.
2-9, Kanda Surugadai, Chiyoda-ku
Tokyo, 101-8911 Japan
http://www.shufunotomo.co.jp/

Printed in China

ISBN4-07-231432-3

Journey to The Ancient Rice Fields

Acknowledgments ·· *6*

Rice Production in Japan ·································· *7*

The Natural Playground ······································ *13*

Cycles of Rice Cultivation —The Metamorphosis— ········ *23*

Gods of The Rice Paddies ································· *37*

Terraced Fields, Natural Dams and Weathers ······ *47*

Shinto Shrines of The Rice Paddies ·················· *55*

Ancestral Burial Grounds ································· *59*

Rice Tasting ·· *81*

Rice Straw ·· *88*

The Future ·· *125*

Acknowledgments

This is my third book to be published by Shufunotomo Co., Ltd. The man behind the scenes responsible for my publications is Mr. Shunichi Kamiya, editor in chief of the International Department. When creating a book he shows great sensitivity and patience, and demonstrates a sharp eye for detail and a love of his work. He cares about perfection and the people he works with, and I thank him from the bottom of my heart for his continued support and wise suggestions.

Another close associate is Mr. Toshiaki Suzuki, who was responsible for the beautiful design of my first book, Japan: The Four Seasons. Again I offer my sincere thanks for his warm cooperation and excellent design for this present publication, Japan: The Ancient Rice Fields.

My thanks to all the people who helped make this publication a reality. To the rice farmers for their sound advice, to the people of Matsunoyama, to my many friends in the Japan Agricultural Association in Tokyo and throughout Japan. And to Fukushima Agricultural Association, with whom I worked in close cooperation over the past 6 years to judge their annual Rice Paddy photo contest. Thank you all for your wonderful kindness.

Finally I wish to thank my wife, Yasuko, and daughter, Hiromi, for their loving support and patience in helping to make all my dreams come true.

Acknowledgments

This is my third book to be published by Shufunotomo Co., Ltd. The man behind the scenes responsible for my publications is Mr. Shu-nichi Kamiya, editor in chief of the International Department. When cre-ating a book he shows great sensitivity and patience, and demon-strates a sharp eye for detail and a love of his work. He cares about perfection and the people he works with, and I thank him from the bot-tom of my heart for his continued support and wise suggestions.

Another close associate is Mr. Toshiaki Suzuki, who was responsi-ble for the beautiful design of my first book, Japan: The Four Seasons. Again I offer my sincere thanks for his warm cooperation and excellent design for this present publication, Japan: The Ancient Rice Fields.

My thanks to all the people who helped make this publication a reality. To the rice farmers for their sound advice, to the people of Mat-sunoyama, to my many friends in the Japan Agricultural Association in Tokyo and throughout Japan. And to Fukushima Agricultural Associa-tion, with whom I worked in close cooperation over the past 6 years to judge their annual Rice Paddy photo contest. Thank you all for your wonderful kindness.

Finally I wish to thank my wife, Yasuko, and daughter, Hiromi, for their loving support and patience in helping to make all my dreams come true.

Journey to The Ancient Rice Fields

Acknowledgments ⋯⋯⋯⋯⋯⋯⋯⋯⋯⋯⋯⋯⋯⋯ *6*

Rice Production in Japan ⋯⋯⋯⋯⋯⋯⋯⋯⋯⋯ *7*

The Natural Playground ⋯⋯⋯⋯⋯⋯⋯⋯⋯⋯ *13*

Cycles of Rice Cultivation —The Metamorphosis— ⋯⋯ *23*

Gods of The Rice Paddies ⋯⋯⋯⋯⋯⋯⋯⋯⋯ *37*

Terraced Fields, Natural Dams and Weathers ⋯⋯ *47*

Shinto Shrines of The Rice Paddies ⋯⋯⋯⋯ *55*

Ancestral Burial Grounds ⋯⋯⋯⋯⋯⋯⋯⋯⋯ *59*

Rice Tasting ⋯⋯⋯⋯⋯⋯⋯⋯⋯⋯⋯⋯⋯⋯⋯ *81*

Rice Straw ⋯⋯⋯⋯⋯⋯⋯⋯⋯⋯⋯⋯⋯⋯⋯ *88*

The Future ⋯⋯⋯⋯⋯⋯⋯⋯⋯⋯⋯⋯⋯⋯ *125*

To Shun Kamiya

Art Direction by Toshiaki Suzuki

Johnny Hymas Photo Office
4274 Minami Yamada-cho
Tsuzuki-ku, Yokohama City
Kanagawa Prefecture
224-0026 Japan
Tel & Fax 81-45-593-0059
http://www.johnny-hymas.net/
e-mail: photo-office@johnny-hymas.net

First printing, 2001

Published by Shufunotomo Co., Ltd.
2-9, Kanda Surugadai, Chiyoda-ku
Tokyo, 101-8911 Japan
http://www.shufunotomo.co.jp/

Printed in China

ISBN4-07-231432-3

JAPAN
The Ancient Rice Fields

Photographs and Text by
Johnny Hymas

SHUFUNOTOMO CO., LTD.
Tokyo, Japan

Rice Production in Japan

It is believed that rice cultivation in Japan started 2,400 years ago, when itinerant Buddhist monks from China brought with them rice seeds and the knowledge of rice paddy cultivation. This was the birth of Japan's rice growing culture, which has continued uninterrupted to the present day.

More recent findings suggest that rice might even have been cultivated in Japan more than 4,000 years ago.

The rice grown in that far distant era was a strain of wild rice or black rice which grew on dry soil, and did not require the complicated husbandry of wet paddy cultivation. Today, there are still some farmers who grow this rice for their own consumption and for sale. When well cooked, the slender, round, purplish black, starchy grains—nearly three-quarters of an inch long—are delicious.

Until a few years ago Japan was the third largest producer of rice in the world. Japan is a small country, and 75 per cent of its land consists of mountain ranges, unsuitable for agricultural use. Of the remaining 25 per cent, 15 per cent is arable. And of this, 60 per cent is used for rice production. Considering that Japan is such a small country and its arable land so limited, it is truly amazing that it was once the third largest producer of rice in the world. Recently, production has fallen because of changing diets and pressure to import rice from overseas, so Japan now ranks eighth in the world. (According to a 1998 survey.)

Apart from the scarcity of arable land, Japan's rice growers are under constant threat from active volcanoes, earthquakes, tidal waves, typhoons, floods and landslides, all of which can ruin crops—and regularly do. No other rice producing country in the world is plagued by so many different natural disasters.

The way arable land is put to use for rice cultivation is highly efficient and competitive: hardly an inch of soil is wasted. Rice growers are specialized farming elite whose ancestors can be traced back for centuries, and their methods of rice cultivation have been passed down from generation to generation. Over the many years farmers have developed their own unique techniques to ensure maximum crop yields. Experimental stations are continuously researching to develop strains of rice for specific regions and for optimum productivity.

Japanese farmers are among the most skilled in the world. They work in small family-run farms, and often do not use the most advanced equipment, but their high levels of efficiency and organization mean they can produce yields higher than countries where farmers have adopted high-tech methods.

It is worth noting that many tropical countries grow two crops of rice each year. The tropics, with their two-season climates (monsoon and summer), their abundance of rain and continuous high temperatures, are ideal for rice cultivation. In most of Japan, on the other hand, because of its four seasons, great fluctuations in temperature, and short rainy season, rice can only be cultivated between April and October, producing just one harvest a year. However, in Kagoshima prefecture and Miyazaki prefecture, which have a warm climate all year round, there are a number of farms growing two crops of rice per year. Overall output is still small, however.

―――― Points of Interest ――――

From the seed beds to harvest, each rice seed planted produces two thousand grains of edible rice—approximately one bowl of rice per seed.

It is astonishing when you stop to consider that since rice was first grown in Japan, perhaps 2,400 years ago, grain has been planted and harvested 2,400 times in the same soil. Year after year, the paddy delivers its crop, and yet the fertility of the soil remains practically unchanged. The nutrients absorbed from the rice paddy during cultivation are reabsorbed by the soil through natural interchange. It is a perfect example of reciprocity in action: the give and take of natural symbiosis.

The fertility of rice paddy soil relies heavily on the water that irrigates it and at the same time feeds it with innumerable microorganisms. The presence of millions of insects and algae all help replenish the soil's composition and fertility. And the water itself binds and holds the soil together, preventing it from becoming dry and arid.

Unlike other crops, rice cultivation does not demand annual crop rotation. This is one of the miracles of rice growing: the yearly transfigurations hardly affect the consistency and fertility of the soil.

Yamaguchi, Yamaguchi Prefecture

Matsunoyama, Niigata Prefecture

Matsunoyama, Niigata Prefecture

Matsunoyama, Niigata Prefecture

Tenri, Nara Prefecture

Sado, Niigata Prefecture

Kiwa, Mie Prefecture

The Natural Playground

One of the most fascinating aspects of rice paddies is their compatibility with wildlife. Over the course of the year, around 200 species of insects, animals, birds, reptiles and fish make the paddies their home, or depend on them for their existence. This figure of 200 is recent data, assessed by the Environment Agency. During the 1960s, however, records show that there were approximately 400 species, but due to vigorous land development, damming of streams and rivers, and growing use of pesticides and artificial fertilizers, half the species are no longer to be found in the rice paddies. Some are close to extinction, or have already become extinct.

When I go on location to photograph rice fields, occasionally I come across children playing there, trying to catch all manner of wildlife, depending on the season—frogs, grasshoppers, butterflies, dragonflies, praying mantises, lizards, beetles, spiders, fresh water crabs. Some children try to catch fish with homemade fishing tackle of bamboo rod and string. Others play with harmless grass snakes, while the more timid scream with fright when they encounter a puff adder. In the evening, children chase fireflies, and others gaze with wonder at the bewitching display of pulsating light.

Some rice paddies play host to wild ducks and their ducklings, who migrate to nest there each year. Beautiful white and gray egrets also find a home in the rice paddies. Centuries ago there were so many of these delicate, graceful birds that they were regarded as gods of the rice paddies. Egrets are shy birds, easily frightened, and they need a quiet, isolated environment. Unfortunately, with the advent of modernization, cities and towns have encroached

further and further on the countryside, bringing noise pollution, and the relentless process of concreting streams and rivers and damming natural ponds and lakes has destroyed habitats. The population of egrets has been drastically depleted. Thirty years ago I remember seeing a great many, but nowadays I see very few, and I fear egrets are becoming an endangered species .

In this age of high-technology recreation, many children are no longer interested in playing in the rice paddies, or communicating with nature and learning the wonders of it. Rice paddies are a natural playground for children, and part of the ancient culture of Japanese folklore and fairy tales. But like much of Japan's precious heritage, rice paddies are becoming a forgotten happiness of a child's life.

Maki, Niigata Prefecture

Kamogawa, Chiba Prefecture

Kamogawa, Chiba Prefecture

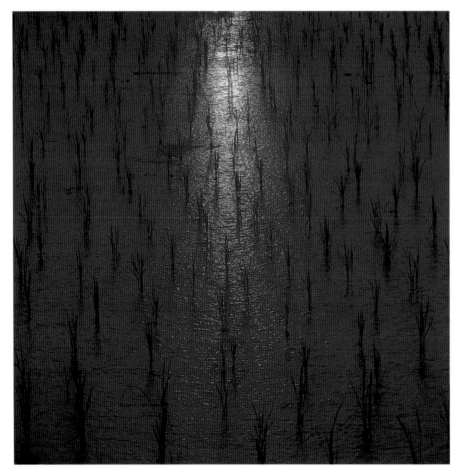

Matsunoyama, Niigata Prefecture

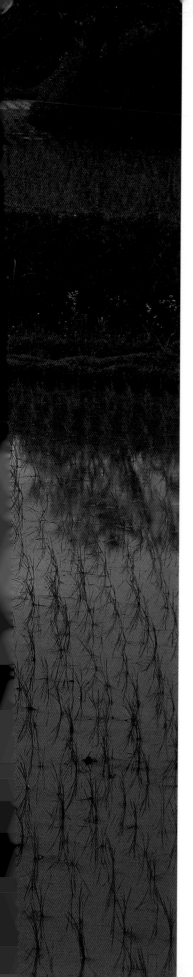

Kamogawa, Chiba Prefecture

Kurama, Kyoto

Sekinomiya, Hyogo Prefecture

Cycles of Rice Cultivation —The Metamorphosis—

The Archipelago of Japan stretches from north to south like a giant bow, extending over a latitude span of 20 degrees and a distance of around 2,000 miles. Hence it is not surprising that there are significant regional differences in temperature, humidity, and precipitation between continental Hokkaido and subtropical Kyushu. Other islands, like Okinawa and Iriomote, have tropical climates and lie at the southern tip of the archipelago. Rice production on both these islands is sparse; the main rice producing areas are Kyushu, Shikoku, Honshu and Hokkaido.

Wide differences in latitude mean that rice growing methods and rice strains vary significantly. Strains of rice grown in the north are not always suitable for the south, and vice versa. Some varieties of rice have been developed specially for rugged mountainous regions, and others for humid low-lying plains. Certain strains have short, hardy stems to guard against strong winds and heavy rains. The northern regions, where winters are long and the spring and summer growing season is short, demand fast-maturing types of rice.

Deep snow often blankets the northern regions from October to April, leaving only a few months for cultivation. It is these regions which interest me most, because it is these cold, snowy districts which produce some of Japan's top grade rice. For example the "Minami Uo Numa" district in Niigata prefecture is famous for its high quality rice and rice-wine. This region has one of the heaviest snowfalls in the country—reaching 4 to 5 meters. How can a locality with one of the highest snowfalls produce the highest quality rice?

Rice growing districts are graded into three quality categories: Grade A, B, and C. Only "Minami Uo Numa" district is allocated "special quality grade A." Its excellence is attributed to several factors. It has a source of fine fresh spring water. Its arable land is perfect for rice cultivation. Extreme weathers influence its soil constitution, in that when snow melts in the spring it feeds the rice paddies with valuable nutrients. And the rice seeds used for planting are top quality. But the most important feature is the people: a dynasty of farmers who for centuries have handed down from generation to generation the secrets of rice husbandry pertaining to their own specific region. Knowing the land thoroughly and understanding its needs is crucial to rice cultivation.

The first step in cultivation is to purchase rice seed from local suppliers, or grow one's own. Either way, the quality of the seeds is paramount.

Not all seeds are fertile: the kernels of some seeds atrophy during storage. There is a traditional way to separate the good seeds from the bad: water is poured into a large vat or container, and an egg is placed on the bottom of the vat; salt is then added to the water in increments until the egg floats to the surface. This indicates that the water has reached perfect buoyancy. At this stage seeds are emptied into the vat; the seeds which float to the surface are infertile, and are scooped up and thrown away. The seeds remaining on the bottom are used for planting. Before planting, the seeds are soaked in water for a short time to help germination. This method of testing the seeds for fertility is archaic, but many farmers still observe the tradition.

This first cycle will take place some time between April and June, depending on the region.

Due to the 20 degree latitude span, planting times from north to south vary a great deal. In the northern regions where snowfalls are heavy, snow is shoveled away from the rice paddies by hand, or removed by bulldozers, to allow planting to begin. Waiting for the snow to melt would take too long, leaving very little time for the rice to grow and mature.

Once the snow has been cleared away, the soil is broken up and turned into a soft loam in preparation for making seedling beds. When the beds are completed, rice seeds are planted in the beds and the beds irrigated with water. The seeds are not totally submerged—they lie in the wet soil near the surface so that the sun's warmth can help them germinate quickly. If the seeds are too deep in the water their germination period is stunted. In extremely cold regions vinyl sheets are arched above the beds to protect the seedlings from frost and sudden snow falls.

The germination period takes only a few days, after which rice seedlings grow and mature. In two to three weeks they are about 9 inches long, and ready for planting. The seedlings are gently lifted from the beds; tied into small bundles and taken to the edge of the rice paddies for planting.

While the seedlings have been maturing in the beds, the farmers have not been idle: they have been preparing their rice paddies for planting. Again the soil is turned over and broken up into loam, and made perfectly flat. Then the paddies are filled with water to a level roughly 3 inches above the paddy mud. This allows the roots of the 9-inch seedlings to be pushed into the wet earth by hand or machine—half of the seedling is submerged, while the other half flourishes above the water.

Planting by hand or machine varies with each region. Some areas are so remote and rugged that tractors and farm machinery are unable to reach them, so all the cultivation is done by hand. Other regions have such deep, muddy paddies that farm machinery sinks into the mud and gets stuck. Some stepped rice paddies are so tiny that machines cannot fit in: generations of farmers determined to make use of the last inch of arable land have created some paddies only a yard in diameter.

Out of long tradition, some farmers still prefer to plant by hand: even though they could use machinery, they choose the old-fashioned way. It is also true that planting by hand gives a higher yield than planting by machine. A farmer friend proved this theory himself; he planted half of one rice paddy by hand and the other half by machine, making sure that he planted exactly the same number of seedlings in each half. After the harvest, he weighed the grain yielded by each half of the paddy. The hand-planted rice seedlings gave 20 lbs. more rice than the half planted by machine.

On the plains where paddies lie flat and cover large areas, nearly all cultivation is done by machinery. These districts are called rice bowls, or rice belts, and it is here where most of Japan's rice is produced.

The rice planting season is a time of great activity, and during this period rice planting festivals and Shinto ceremonies are widely performed, to implore the gods for a bumper harvest, and to protect the farmers from accidents and sickness.

When the rice-planting season ends, the mon-

soon season begins. This rainy period lasts for six weeks from June to mid-July. The monsoon is the life-blood of the rice. During this period the rice gains strength and flourishes; without a prolific rainy season the rice plants may become dry and stunted, and the grains will not develop fully.

In mid-July the borders of the rice paddies are covered with luxuriant grasses, burgeoning plants and flowers. To my mind, this is one of the most enchanting times of year. The myriad of plants and flowers make it seem as if each rice paddy is growing its own flower garden.

In mid-summer the rice grows lush and prolific; everywhere you turn the paddies are a brilliant emerald green. It is also the time when ears of rice manifest themselves and burst into bloom.

When I first started photographing rice fields I had no idea that rice did actually flower. When you look at rice fields in full bloom, the petals are so tiny they are hardly visible. You have to look closely to see their delicate white blossoms, sprouting from the grain husks like dainty snowflakes.

The length of time the flowers bloom is quite short—only a matter of hours. The best time to photograph them is early morning when it is cool and the blossoms are moist and fresh. By midday the heat from the sun dries the fragile petals, and they soon wilt and die. If the weather is cool and rainy, the blooms can last a couple of days in the moist air.

When I want to photograph rice blossoms, I usually telephone farmer acquaintances and ask their advice for the best time to catch the rice in full bloom. If they advise me that the morning of the following day is the best bet, I leave immediately and try to arrive before daybreak: I should have a chance to photograph the sunrise, as well as catching the rice flowers at their fresh, early-morning best, while they are still covered in dew.

Because the petals are so small I use a macro-lens, or close-up attachments. If I were to use a standard lens, the petals would be scarcely discernible through the camera view-finder. To get the best pictures, I use a plus 5 or a plus 8 close-up attachment, or a 200mm macro-lens. These lenses and attachments are also ideal for photographing tiny insects.

After the rice flowers have bloomed, the transition to late summer is almost imperceptible—like growing old. The colors of the rice fields change from light ocher to deep gold. The time has now come to prepare for reaping. This means weeding the paddies, draining their water, cutting back the vegetation on the borders and burning it, or using it for compost.

Weeding is done so that reaping machines do not pick up weeds during cutting—weeds can be troublesome when separating ears of rice from the stalks. Draining off the water lets the paddies dry out and the soil harden, and makes the paddies accessible to heavy reaping machines. It also helps the rice to dry out and ripen more quickly.

During this busy period, the rice reaches its full maturity. Only a farmer can judge when the rice is ripe. They break off an ear of rice, rub off the husk in their hands, then pop a few grains in their mouths and bite it to taste whether the kernel has fully matured. When they nod their heads and say "*Ja, hajimeyo ka* (let's begin!)," that is the signal for harvest to begin. For me, it is the first sign of autumn.

Harvesting is a period of intense activity, back-breaking-labor and sweat. From germination to maturation, the rice has developed in its own time, but now the moment has come to reap. The process is quick and efficient, and the golden harvest disappears from the paddies almost like magic.

Some farmers brandish their ancient sickles and reap by hand. On the vast plains large combine harvesters strip the paddies bare in no time and carry their grain to warehouses to be dried by machine. The mountainous areas and many small farms hang their rice to mellow in the sun and wind, on frames of all shapes and sizes. Each district has its own method of frame design, handed down from ancestor to ancestor. North, south, east and west are all different, but typical of how ancient Japan dried its rice centuries ago, with each regional style influenced by the local environment and resources.

In Niigata prefecture there is a rice belt called Niigata Heya. It stretches for miles and miles in all directions, and its rice output is enormous. Many years ago, when I first came to Japan, I visited the district often, but sadly never shot any photographs. What interested me most about the area was the "*Hasaki no Ki*," or in English, "drying trees."

"Drying trees" were planted on the borders of the rice paddies for the specific purpose of attaching drying frames to them during harvesting. Thousands of these trees used to surround the rice paddies. Throughout the year the trees changed color with the seasons and were eye-catchingly beautiful. They were even a tourist attraction in the area.

I am sad to say that these old trees no longer exist. They were cut down because they interfered with tractors and crop spraying by airplane. The trees to me were an agricultural treasure and should have been left as a reminder and a monument to Japan's ancient rice culture.

It takes rice roughly ten to fifteen days to dry in the sun and wind. Over this time, the rice matures into a deep brownish gold. I think this is when rice looks most appetizing—like ripe juicy fruit hanging from the branches of a tree.

Once the rice has dried and ripened, the next stage is to separate the husks from the grains, whether by machine or hand. Machine threshing takes only a few hours, while separating the husks from the grains manually is archaic and time consuming, but out of long tradition some farmers still perform this arduous task. They cover the ground with a large canvas sheet, and put mature ears of rice on the sheet. Then two, three or four farmers, working in rhythm, beat the rice with wooden clubs attached to stems of bamboo with ropes or chains. When beating the rice there is a whiplash effect between the bamboo stem and the club; this gives extra power to the club, but conserves the farmers' strength.

When the grain has been separated from the husks, it is put into sacks and carried to warehouses and silos for storage. The husks are burned, and ashes from the husks are used as fertilizer the following year.

Once the grain is safely stored away, harvest festivals are performed throughout the land with great vigor and spirited celebration. Shinto rites are observed, to thank the gods for another good harvest. And as the harvest moon wanes, another season begins.

   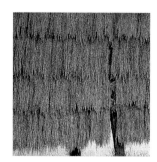

It is now late autumn and the rice paddies can appear barren and spent—but not so. They carry an aura of aged fertility like the weather beaten face of an old man, battered by the seasons and wrinkled with time, but still powerful and full of energy and life.

The rice paddies are now stripped of their bounty, and only the withering rice stumps remain, which will be plowed into the paddy as compost in the spring.

In the northern regions during late autumn, the weather is unpredictable and changes quickly. The paddies go through many changes—some mornings they are blanketed with heavy ground frosts; the next day comes the first snowfall, and the following day perhaps rain, and after the rain, eddying mists, which hover above the paddies as if they were a primeval marshland. Each day paints a different picture, but gradually the days grow colder and colder until heavy snowfalls carpet the land and only one picture remains—winter white.

For me winter is not the end but the beginning. When deep snow falls and covers the paddies, they go into hibernation, resting to gain strength for the next year's growth. Insects go into hiding and winter sleep. In the depths of the paddies there are all kinds of chrysalis, cocoons and eggs waiting to hatch in the spring.

Birds which made a temporary home in the paddies have migrated. Animals and reptiles have gone into hibernation. All is silent, only the winter winds voice their icy presence. Districts isolated deep in the mountains stock up for winter and collect firewood from mountain forests.

During the long winters, farmers clear away the snow from the roofs of their dwellings and cut pathways in the snow with their shovels. Snow sometimes piles up 5 meters high. In some regions the snow is so deep that only the windows and doors of dwellings are visible; the rest of the structure is buried under voluminous piles of snow. In some rice growing areas of Hokkaido the temperature can drop to minus 40°C.

Photographing the northern climes in winter is a lesson in survival. Without a hardy four-wheel drive vehicle and snow chains, most roads are impassable. When I try to reach the best locations for shooting, snow shoes are essential, or I could be stumbling through snowdrifts 10 meters deep. It is a harrowing experience suddenly to slip into a deep ditch, hidden by a snow drift. Even wearing snowshoes, you can find yourself waist deep in icy water with a gigantic roof of snow above your head.

When on location in mercilessly cold regions I try to learn from farmers how they cope with such unforgiving elements. All I have learned is that the farmers are a breed of people whose ancestors have endured in the same environment for centuries, and acclimatized themselves to coexist with the forces of nature, no matter how hostile they may be. At the same time they have discovered the secrets of subsisting from nature without destroying it. These are the people I respect most, for they have great patience and dignity, and represent the true soul of Japan.

In the northern regions winter starts in late October and ends in March or April. Then the cycle starts all over again.

The beginning and the end are as one—there is no demarcation line. THIS IS NATURE.

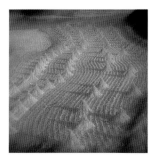

Kamogawa, Chiba Prefecture

Omura, Nagasaki Prefecture

Kiyosato, Niigata Prefecture

Tanagura, Fukushima Prefecture

Kamogawa, Chiba Prefecture

Matsunoyama, Niigata Prefecture

Koshokushi, Nagano Prefecture

Matsunoyama, Niigata Prefecture

Gods of The Rice Paddies

Around three hundred years ago, in the Kyushu areas of Kagoshima and Miyazaki prefectures, the local farmers, with the help of stonemasons, made effigies to represent "gods of the rice paddies." In Japanese, the gods are called *"ta no kami-sama."*

The stone effigies were fashioned in such a way that half the sculpture resembled a penis, while the other half is a carving of a woman. The combination of male and female in one sculpture was created to represent fertility.

The farmers prayed to these stone gods for good harvests, and for protection from sickness and injury. They also entreated the gods to spare them from ravaging typhoons, which more often than not hit during harvest time. It is said that the main reason the stone gods were created in the first place was to protect crops from devastating typhoons and hurricanes. Even today some farmers still pray to the *"ta no kami-sama,"* begging that their crops and homes should not be destroyed by remorseless weather. Often when I speak with Kagoshima and Miyazaki farmers they talk about the heartbreak of losing crops during harvest, after the months of hard work spent tending them.

Kagoshima recently suffered horrific damage from torrential rains and hurricane-force winds. Rice-growing localities were devastated, homes were destroyed and lives were lost. Until the Taisho era there were hundreds of *"ta no kami-sama"* standing on the borders of rice paddies, acting as their guardians—practically every farmer had his own. The size and shape of the effigies varied greatly. Some were small, and were often carried home and put in a prominent place for worship during the winter months. When rice planting started in the spring, they were brought back to the paddies as their guardians.

Today there are very few of the rice-paddy gods remaining. Many have been stolen or destroyed, and because of mechanization farmers have hauled them home permanently, or taken them to quiet locations where they do not get in the way of cultivation.

Out of long tradition, festivals in honor of the rice-paddy gods are still performed, especially at harvest time, to thank the gods for their help with the crops. The stone carvings are an integral part of local wedding ceremonies, and during the celebrations they are put in a place of honor, for the bride and bridegroom to pray to for a happy marriage and strong, healthy offspring.

When I first saw the gods of the rice paddies, I was surprised by their strong masculine and feminine aspects. They carry an aura of inexplicable power, as if they really do protect the rice paddies and help make them fertile.

The statues are now weather-beaten and covered with moss and mildew. The carved contours of the faces on many effigies have almost worn away, and the more weathered the statues become, the more they gain a sphinx-like air of purpose to their ancient lives.

Kurama, Kyoto

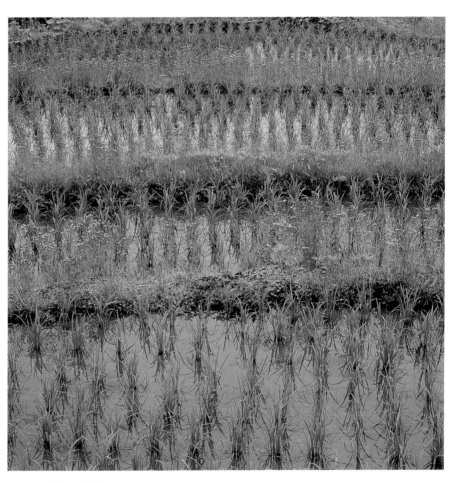

Kiyosato, Niigata Prefecture

Shonai, Oita Prefecture

Matsunoyama, Niigata Prefecture

Koshakushi, Nagano Prefecture

Matsunoyama, Niigata Prefecture

Matsunoyama, Niigata Prefecture

Matsunoyama, Niigata Prefecture

Sekinomiya, Hyogo Prefecture

Terraced Fields, Natural Dams and Weathers

Many rice paddies in Japan cling to steep mountainsides, and have endured so long in the mountain terrain that they have become a part of the ecology of the mountains that host them. When I look closely at the rice fields, they give a forceful impression that mother nature created the rice paddies when she gave birth to the mountains—the paddies seem to have always been there.

All the ancient rice fields of Japan were hewn from the earth with primitive tools—a formidable task, especially on steep and rocky mountain slopes. There were no bulldozers or hydraulic shovels in those days, so farmers had to dig out the terraced paddies by hand, following the natural contours of the mountain.

Because there were no water pumps they had to consider how to make use of water from mountain streams and springs. The rice paddies were built to allow water from the mountain to flow by gravity from paddy to paddy, through sloping ducts and ditches. The skill of these long-forgotten farmers in manipulating and controlling nature's resources, with only the barest essentials at their disposal, is quite awe-inspiring.

When I think of the rugged, unyielding mountain environment, and the great difficulty of capturing and using water, I see the ancient paddies as agricultural works of art and believe they should be preserved as natural monuments for future generations. For they are one of Japan's most valuable legacies, not just as a scenic memory, but as a reminder that these ancient paddies have helped sustain the nation for centuries, or even millennia.

During the rice planting season and monsoon, the rice paddies are brimming with water. Water covers roughly 60 per cent of all agricultural land. The monsoon season lasts for six weeks, from early June to mid July, and the average monthly rainfall during this period is 1600mm.

During the six-week rainy season, rice paddies act as natural dams and prevent widespread flooding. The paddies collect water from the heavy rains and then drain off the water through ducts, pipes and ditches into streams, rivers and canals—siphoning off the deluge and keeping water levels to a minimum. As well as acting as natural dams, when they are full of water the rice paddies have a direct influence on the atmosphere: they cause high humidity, mists, thunderstorms, winds and precipitation.

If you can imagine a small mountainous island country, with more than half of its arable land covered with water, it is not difficult to see what a dynamic effect the wet rice paddies can have on local weather.

Ohara, Chiba Prefecture

Tono, Iwate Prefecture

Noto Peninsula, Ishikawa Prefecture

Mogami, Yamagata Prefecture

Kamogawa, Chiba Prefecture

Tono, Iwate Prefecture

Shinto Shrines of The Rice Paddies

Japan had a feudal system which lasted for centuries, and during that time landowners and tenant farmers built Shinto shrines in their rice growing territories. The shrines acted as border posts or demarcation markers for each district. There were literally thousands of these Shinto shrines dotted all over Japan. The farmers used the shrines for worship, festivals, weddings, christenings, funerals and various other Shinto rites.

Today, many of these ancient shrines still exist, although, sadly, many of them are unkempt and dilapidated, almost eaten up by the pervading undergrowth where rice cultivation has long ceased. Some shrines are well cared for and are still part of community life, used for all kinds of ceremonies.

The charm of the shrines is that they are found in the center of rice growing localities—at the edge of rice paddies, or in the middle of them. Some can be found hidden away in bamboo groves and copses, at the foot of tree-covered hillocks, or on top of them. These archaic structures are an inherent part of Japan's rice growing culture.

The Shinto religion is intimately linked to rice cultivation—they have been interwoven over the centuries. Fertility rites are tied up with the fertility of rice cultivation. The Shimenawa, a thick rope that hangs in front of Shinto shrines and their Torii gates, is hand-woven from rice straw. At the beginning of each year a fresh Shimenawa rope is woven from the straw of the recent rice harvest to replace the old one. This is an ancient custom, dating back many centuries. The Shimenawa rope, when hung over the threshold of the shrine's main building of worship, is supposed to act as a barrier to protect evil spirits from entering the shrine. It is a boundary between good and evil.

Five minutes' walk from my home there is an old shrine called Yamata Jinja*. To reach the shrine one must climb a hundred steep steps, then walk along a stone pathway which cuts through a bamboo grove and a thick copse of trees. When I am not on location, I climb the hundred steps and visit the shrine each day. Out of courtesy I stand below the Shimenawa rope, throw a few coins into a large wooden money box, ring the suzu bell which hangs below the Shimenawa rope at the portal of the shrine's building (this lets the gods know I am there). I then clap my hands three times, bow my head and make a prayer, which is the customary form of worship at a Shinto shrine.

Yamata Jinja is a beautifully located shrine, which stands on top of a high hillock. On a clear day you can see Mount Fuji.

Yamata Shrine is a treasured relic of yesteryear, somehow surviving in the midst of aggressive urban development. But the steps that lead to the shrine are destined to be bulldozed into oblivion, so that the road at the foot of the shrine can be widened.

Not so long ago, the shrine was surrounded by wide plains of rice paddies, stretching out in every direction as far as the eye could see. The shrine was an integral part of this wonderful rice-growing area, and was used by the farming community for all kinds of events and ceremonies. An old farmer friend of mine, who lives close by, showed me some sepia photographs of the rice paddies, taken from the top of Yamata Jinja's hillock during the Meiji Era. It was stunning to see the typical Japanese landscape of that period. The old photographs showed what was once the "true heart of Japan," and it was painful to see how this beautiful area looked a century ago, when I am only too familiar with today's ugly landscape.

* "Yamata Jinja" in English means "mountain rice paddy shrine." *Yama* is mountain, ta is rice paddy, and *jinja* is shrine.

Matsunoyama, Niigata Prefecture

Miki, Kagawa Prefecture

Ancestral Burial Grounds

The cremating and enshrining of deceased family members in ancestral burial grounds in the center of rice paddies or in the immediate vicinity of them, is a custom which dates back to when rice was first cultivated over two thousand years ago. Even today this custom is still observed.

Many burial grounds are so ancient that the present day descendants have lost track of their age. Names and dates on the tombstones have been eroded with the passing of time, and some have crumbled out of all recognition.

Municipal offices keep records of land ownership and births, deaths and marriages. Records, however, do not go back far enough to reveal the age of the burial grounds or the age of the rice paddies that host them. If you could identify the dates carved on the oldest gravestones you would uncover both the age of the burial grounds and the rice paddies at the same time.

In some cases, the expertise of an archaeologist is needed to work out the origin and age of some burial grounds, and once that has been assessed, one can determine the age of the rice paddies.

When photographing ancient paddies and their related artifacts,

it is important to know how long they have existed, for it teaches you their profound historical significance. Japan's culture is rooted in the rice paddies. Everything connected to rice cultivation depicts a story of man's deep relationship with his land. He is born of the land, he cultivates it, and when he dies, he returns to it.

I remember some years ago when on photo location in Nara prefecture, I stopped to ask an aged farmer who was reaping the harvest how old his paddies were. Looking at me with a sarcastic grin on his face, and in a local twang that I could barely understand, he said: "I think they have been here from the beginning of time–like myself!" He was 100 years old, and looking at his weathered and gnarled features more closely, I was inclined to believe him!

Teshima, Kagawa Prefecture

Tono, Iwate Prefecture

Matsunoyama, Niigata Prefecture

Yamatsuri, Fukushima Prefecture

Shirakawa, Gifu Prefecture

Noto Peninsula, Ishikawa Prefecture

Matsunoyama, Niigata Prefecture

Kamogawa, Chiba Prefecture

Shirakawa, Gifu Prefecture

Ohara, Chiba Prefecture

Matsumoto, Nagano Prefecture

Chiyoda, Ibaraki Prefecture

Ohara, Chiba Prefecture

Chiyoda, Ibaraki Prefecture

Oshima, Niigata Prefecture

Gasho, Gifu Prefecture

Matsunoyama, Niigata Prefecture

Matsunoyama, Niigata Prefecture

Tosa, Kochi Prefecture

Togakushi, Nagano Prefecture

Tosa, Kochi Prefecture

Matsumoto, Nagano Prefecture

Matsunoyama, Niigata Prefecture

Matsunoyama, Niigata Prefecture

Rice Tasting

In Japan there are many varieties of rice, the most popular of which is a strain called koshihikari. Its popularity is due to its characteristic sweet aroma, and the taste and quality of its grains when cooked. Among the masses of people who eat rice as their staple food there are some who are connoisseurs and can taste minute distinctions between different varieties of rice—somewhat like expert wine-tasters.

Trying to describe variations in the taste of rice is not easy. Some people have a sensitive palate; others do not. When I first came to Japan all rice tasted the same to me, but now, after thirty years, I have acquired a discerning taste. I eat mainly Japonica non-glutinous brown rice, known in Japanese as genmai. The reason I eat it is to keep my weight down, and improve health. Many Japanese sportsmen eat brown rice to increase their power and stamina. Brown rice takes some getting used to; it is harder to chew than standard white rice, and has a bland taste, but after a while you grow accustomed to it, and if you persevere, it does help keep you slim and healthy.

Most rice grown in Japan is related to a "mother rice" called Japonica. Offshoots from this strain have different grain names, but are still of Japonica origin. If you compare Japonica rice with the rice of other Asian countries, its grains are shorter, the cooked rice is more glutinous and sticky, and it is also more nutritious than long-grain rice.

I remember watching a television program, some years ago, which compared Japonica rice with rice grown in south-east Asia. To make the program, the director enlisted 24 university students, of both sexes, in an experiment.

Over a six-month period half the students ate Japonica rice and the other half ate a long-grain variety. Both groups of students ate exactly the same food and exactly the same quantity of rice, which, if I remember correctly, was nine bowls a day.

So that the experiment could produce accurate data, the participants were carefully selected according to weight and body metabolism. All the students were weighed before the experiment, and again after six months of the rice diet. The students who ate the long-grain rice hardly gained weight at all; the students who ate the Japonica rice put on considerable amounts of weight.

A key factor, which influences quality and affects taste, is the water used in the paddies. Many farmers use natural springs and mountain streams for irrigation.

The water from these sources carries valuable minerals, nutrients and micro-organisms which aid growth and affect taste and quality.

During the past thirty years—all the time I have lived in Japan—the damming of rivers, construction of concrete ditches and use of steel pipes for irrigation have increased alarmingly. What were once beautiful natural ditches and streams—brimming over with all manner of wild life—are now eyesores, devoid of organic structures and water-life. At the same time, these concrete and metal waterways destroy the ancient grace of the rice paddies, and ruin the quality and taste of rice.

Another influence on flavor is the use of natural compost rather than artificial fertilizers. Some farmers reject chemical pesticides in favor of planting various species of pest-repellent flowers on the borders of their rice paddies. The effect of this natural husbandry is to improve both quality and taste.

Many farmers follow the tradition of hanging freshly-harvested rice to dry in the sun and wind, which gives the cooked rice a mellow flavor. Other farmers dry their rice by machine, which is quick and efficient, but the taste is never as good as naturally dried rice.

As I have traveled through Japan, I have made friends with many farmers whose rice paddies I often photograph. Each year they send me gifts of their home-grown rice, produced entirely by natural cultivation. I feel truly fortunate in being able to eat such purebred rice, as the quality and flavor is superb.

Ohara, Kyoto

Togakushi, Nagano Prefecture

Kiyosato, Niigata Prefecture

Iiyama, Nagano Prefecture

Iiyama, Nagano Prefecture

Matsunoyama, Niigata Prefecture

Iiyama, Nagano Prefecture

Kitakata, Fukushima Prefecture

Tosa, Kochi Prefecture

Owani, Aomori Prefecture

Ueda, Nagano Prefecture

Togakushi, Nagano Prefecture

Rice Straw

Tatami (straw mats)

The floors of traditional Japanese rooms are laid with *tatami* mats, which are stuffed with rice straw and covered with woven rushes (*igusa*). Standard *tatami* sizes vary from region to region. In the Kyoto area, one *tatami* measures 1.91m by 0.95m; in the Nagoya area a mat is 1.82m by 0.91m, and in Tokyo, 1.76m by 0.88m. The average thickness of a *tatami* is 6cm.

A single *tatami* mat is called *ichi-jo*. Japanese style rooms are measured by the number of *tatami* covering a floor. For example a three *tatami* (*san-jo*) room is quite small, but an eighteen mat (*juhachi-jo*) is large. If you tell a Japanese person the number of *tatami* in a room, they can immediately picture the size of a room. There are also half-size mats called *han-jo*, and three-quarter sizes called *daime-datami*, which are used specifically for Tea Ceremony rooms. The history of *tatami* is thought to date back to the Heian era (794-1185). In early days, it is thought *tatami* mats were used singly and did not cover the entire floor surface of a room.

Wara Buki (thatched roofs)

Rice straw is a by-product which has many uses. In ancient times, and even today, rice straw is a valuable commodity for the rice grower's mode of life. Roofs of houses, barns and sheds are thatched with it. Now, the practice is gradually dying out, but out of long tradition some districts still build thatched roofs to try to maintain the ancient beauty of their surroundings.

Wara Ningyo (straw dolls)

Dolls and all sorts of others toys can be made from rice straw. The toy-making tradition dates back to the Jomon period (roughly 10,000BC to 300BC). Today, straw folk dolls and toys are still made by artisans, and are popular as souvenirs, ornaments and playthings for children.

Shimenawa (straw rope for Shinto rites)

Shimenawa is a special kind of cord, plaited and twisted together from strands of rice straw, which has particular significance in Japan's native Shinto religion. *Shimenawa* can be vast, or miniature. *Shimenawa* is used to mark sacred places and protect them from evil spirits. In Shinto shrines, it is hung at the front of the main worship halls (*haiden*), in front of the alter, and across the entrance gate (*torii*). The rope is also draped around ancient trees that are regarded as revered abodes of the divine.

Large rocks, where deities are thought to sit, can also be hung with *shimenawa*.

Nawa (ordinary straw rope or string)

Nawa, plaited by hand or machine, has long been used for all manner of farming jobs, but recently nylon rope has become more common, and straw rope is gradually disappearing.

Hoki (straw brooms)

Brooms made from straw are still popular today, and can easily be found in hardware shops. *Hoki* are cheap, attractive, easy to use and keep clean.

Mino (straw raincoats)

Before Western-style raincoats reached Japan, on wet days people reached for *mino*—coverings made of woven rice straw, which have been used in Japan since ancient times. Designs vary depending on the area where the *mino* is made. In the cold north or warm south the mino is constructed differently to cope with icy or mild weathers. Today the *mino* is rarely used. In remote regions, however, deep in the mountains, farmers still make and wear the *mino* for rainy and snowy weathers. Although it is made of straw, it is highly effective at keeping out rain and snow.

Waraji (traditional straw sandals)

Woven straw soles are tied to the feet with thongs of rice straw. In olden times *waraji* were used throughout Japan, and worn when taking a long journey on foot. They are light, easy to carry in travelers' bags, and easily disposed of. Today, straw sandals are still made in some areas, and worn by farmers or used for decoration.

Tawara (large straw sacks)

Tawara are used to carry and store rice and many other farm products.

Kamasu (Straw bags and sacks)

Made by folding a length of straw matting, sewing up the sides and making it into a bag. *Kamasu* are used for transporting grain, coal, fertilizers, salt and other commodities. Smaller, finely woven *kamasu* were once used as purses and tobacco pouches, but the introduction of paper and plastic bags and sacks has led to a drastic decline in use of *kamasu*.

Esa (animal fodder)

Rice straw is chopped into small pieces and stored in silos for use in winter months to feed livestock.

Hiryo (composted farm manure)

In ancient times, raw materials such as bamboo, timber, stone, mud and clay, resins, reeds, rice straw and water, were some of the basic elements with which man maintained his life. He took from the land only what he needed. His survival was according to nature's law, coexisting in harmony with nature, and without despoiling it.

Taisho, Kochi Prefecture

Asuka, Nara Prefecture

Yusuhara, Kochi Prefecture

Kamogawa, Chiba Prefecture

Minami-Okuni, Kumamoto Prefecture

Nomura, Ehime Prefecture

Yusuhara, Kochi Prefecture

Ogawa, Nagano Prefecture

Miyasa, Nagano Prefecture

Yusuhara, Kochi Prefecture

Oshima, Niigata Prefecture

Matsunoyama, Niigata Prefecture

Kamogawa, Chiba Prefecture

Togakushi, Nagano Prefecture

Koshoku, Nagano Prefecture

Uchiko, Ehime Prefecture

Matsunoyama, Niigata Prefecture

Koshoku, Nagano Prefecture

Matsunoyama, Niigata Prefecture

Tajima, Fukushima Prefecture

Togakushi, Nagano Prefecture

Hakuba, Nagano Prefecture

Tajima, Fukushima Prefecture

Matsunoyama, Niigata Prefecture

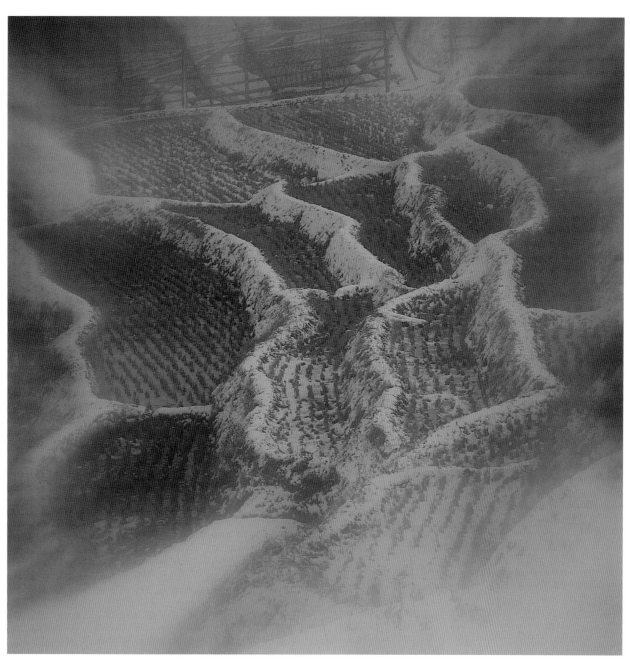

Noto Peninsula, Ishikawa Prefecture

Uchiko, Ehime Prefecture

Matsunoyama, Niigata Prefecture

Toya, Hokkaido

Ouchi, Fukushima Prefecture

Bifuka, Hokkaido

Johana, Toyama Prefecture

Matsunoyama, Niigata Prefecture

The Future

Rice growing in Japan is affected by many factors: some ancient, some modern, some good and some bad. During the past fifty years, however, the bad influences have come to outweigh the good ones considerably. The future of rice cultivation as we know it today is now at risk.

The most pressing problem is manpower. Even when I first came to Japan, thirty years ago, I did not see many young people working in the rice paddies; most were old and middle aged. During the past three decades, the elderly of that era have passed away, and the middle-aged farmers have now grown old. They may be the last in their line of Japan's rice-growing dynasty. When these aged farmers pass away, their land will become idle, as most of their children and grandchildren have for-

saken their roots. They choose to live in the towns or cities, and have no interest in agriculture. From childhood, they have been exposed to the seductive propaganda of modern, urban life. From the media, they develop an image of a high-tech, sophisticated society and want to be part of it. The whole idea of farming, to the younger generation, is boring, arduous and dirty. They have no desire to become farmers, which to them is the same as saying country bumpkins. This attitude is widespread: children have been robbed of their sense of depth about the important things in life, and lost respect for their ancient origins.

Due to dwindling manpower, farming associations, local governments and the farmers themselves are deeply worried about this situation. The greatest threat is that if there is a drastic shortage of man power or, worse still, no manpower at all, large conglomerates may try to take control of the unoccupied rice growing areas. They will depend on biotechnology and mass production, which will dramatically alter the face of Japan's countryside. Huge tracts of land will be blighted by vinyl houses and ugly concrete structures designed to grow engineered crops, using high-tech agricultural methods, with the minimum of manpower! If this nightmare comes true, what were once the heartlands of Japan — its enchanting countryside — will be desecrated by, as always, the lust for money.

This will not happen overnight. It will be slow and insidious, and by the end of this century or the next, the

Japanese countryside will be unrecognizable.

Another detrimental element affecting Japanese rice production is imported rice, which is cheaper than rice grown in Japan. Price-conscious consumers buy it, but this harms domestic rice growers by creating an oversupply that can only be remedied by cutbacks in production. Together with diminishing manpower, this problem is causing havoc in the rice-growing community. A huge proportion of rice-producing land—roughly 37.5 percent—is now lying idle and unproductive.

There are many political factors exacerbating these difficulties, especially friction with foreign governments, who demand the right to export their agricultural products to Japan. But it does not make sense to import rice into a country that already has more than enough. It threatens the livelihood of rice farmers, and reduces the value of Japan's rice-growing culture to an insultingly low level.

I believe the heritage of rice cultivation in Japan is priceless, and should be revered as such. Rice farming should be rigorously supported and protected from the ravages of irrational, mindless progress.

The Environment Agency recently designated over a hundred rice paddy locations throughout Japan as cultural assets, to be preserved unchanged in their present state. Unfortunately, however, only the rice paddies themselves have been awarded this distinction. The areas around them, or even right next to them, are not protected by the new designation. The paradox in this is that because the paddies have been nominated as cultural assets, some local governments are trying to improve facilities in the surrounding areas, to cater for tourists who may wish to view the historical paddies. They are building car parks and public toilets, and erecting large billboards with written explanations about the history of the paddies.

One local government even has plans to build a restaurant for light refreshments, a car park and a public toilet right next to a beautiful cluster of ancient paddies. To do this, they intend to fell a bamboo thicket that blends in perfectly with the rustic atmosphere of the rice paddies.

In other "protected" locations, I was shocked to discover that the ancient footpaths crisscrossing the paddies are being reconstructed with concrete, to allow tourists to view the paddies without getting their shoes dirty or their high heels stuck in the mud. The new concrete paths look ugly and clash with the ancient grace of the paddies. I wish local governments could understand this.

To preserve a natural area properly, one must not allow any changes that will ruin its ancient quality. Catering for tourists is defiling the purity and dignity of Japan's rice-growing heritage. If tourists want to visit these venerable landmarks, they should show their respect and see their journey as not just a sightseeing jaunt but something much more profound. Rice paddies are more sacred than any shrine or temple, for they were once the life force of Japan.

Farmers and their land should not be downgraded to mere tourist attractions. Japan's rice growing culture deserves much more esteem.

In England there is an environmental and cultural preservation association called the National Trust. Its role is to protect the country's physical history: its ancient villages and towns, forests and fields, historical monuments and buildings, and natural habitats. The association is painstakingly rigorous with its preservation laws and strict in upholding them. Districts that are designated as cultural assets are vigorously protected. Whole villages and towns that are safeguarded by the National Trust are not allowed to build modern architecture in the protected areas. Even the people who own ancient dwellings are banned from altering the interior or exterior in any way. They must seek permission just to hammer in nails, or repaint a wall. When people buy these ancient houses, the purchase contract includes a special clause which stipulates that they are not allowed to remodel anything. The houses are so captivatingly rustic, inside and out, that no sensible person would wish to alter them anyway.

Telegraph poles and electric pylons are nowhere to be seen in British conservation areas. When visiting these places it is like a time slip— they are so beautifully preserved that they can look exactly as they did five or six hundred years ago.

I wish Japan had its own strict conservation group. It might have some chance of putting the brakes on the country's headlong rush for "progress," which serves only to disfigure its beautiful countryside.

During the past half century. Japan has gone through one of its most dynamic periods of change, and is now on the brink of even greater change. But progressing blindly, with no thought of safeguarding its unique culture and philosophies, will deprive the country of its values and identity. Preserving the past is the cornerstone of building the future and Japan's rice-growing culture is a vital part of the country's foundations.

Today I learned that, due to exceptionally fine weather this summer, the rice crop is forecast to exceed all expectations and create a substantial surplus. Accordingly, the government has instructed certain areas to destroy a portion of their crops while they are maturing in the paddies. In Japanese, this is called "*ao ta gari*," or "to reap rice when it is still green" This wasteful procedure not only hurts the starving millions of the world, but causes much anger and resentment among the farmers who have labored to grow the rice.

Considering that there are countries in the world, especially in Africa, suffering from grievous famine, the surplus of rice— which is due to be destroyed— could be a humanitarian godsend for the starving people, and the children dying of malnutrition.

Japan already donates much of its surplus rice and other commodities to countries devastated by natural disasters and famine, but even so, I feel that to destroy crops because they will create a

glut should not be the unethical trend of the twenty-first century. Every surplus grain of rice or ounce of food should be distributed to the countries where it is needed, or stored for the future, in case of natural or man-made catastrophes. We can never know what the future holds.

The saying, "waste not, want not," in this day and age should be observed as a moral imperative. Governments who have the money and power should also remember that where there is a compassionate will, there is a way.

My hope for the future is that there will be much conscientious study and thoughtful consideration before any drastic changes are made. Japan has rapidly developed into a major industrialized nation, but to achieve this, it has paid an enormous price. This should not happen to Japan's legacy of traditional farming: it is too precious.

To grow one ton of rice requires
2000 tons of precious water.